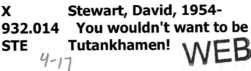

1323 BC

Tutankhamen dies unexpectedly at the age of 18 or 19. Ay becomes pharaoh and arranges Tutankhamen's burial.

English archaeologist Howard Carter discovers the long-lost tomb of Tutankhamen. The contents of the tomb capture the world's imagination.

March 1323 BC

Tutankhamen's funeral takes place in The Valley of the Kings.

Map of Ancient Egypt

Egypt is a country located between the northeast corner of Africa and the southwest corner of Asia, much of it within the Nile Valley. At roughly 4,130 miles (6,650 kilometers) in length, the Nile is the longest river in the world. In ancient Egypt, the river was used to transport goods and merchandise throughout the continent.

Memphis was the original capital city of ancient Egypt. It was an important cultural center. It is where the pharaohs had many of the major pyramids built to preserve their memory. Memphis was also home to the great temple of Ptah, an Egyptian god of craftsmen.

Thebes became the capital city later. On the opposite bank of the Nile from Thebes was the Necropolis, or "city of the dead," which contained the royal tombs.

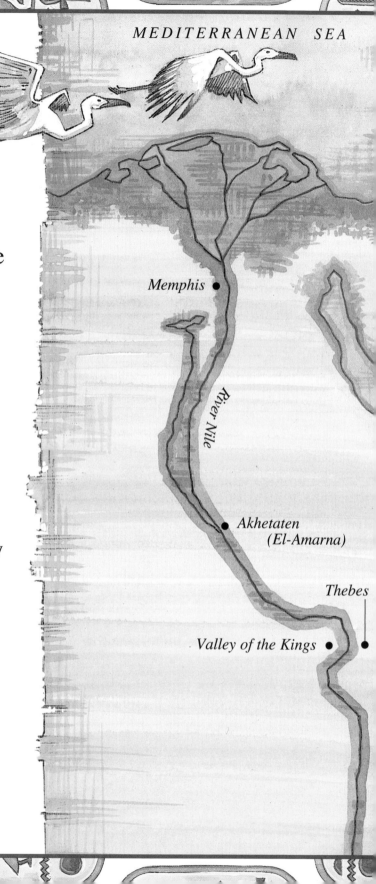

MEDITERRANEAN SEA

Memphis

River Nile

Akhetaten
(El-Amarna)

Thebes

Valley of the Kings

Author:
David Stewart has written many
nonfiction books for children. He lives in
Brighton, England, with his family.

Artist:
David Antram was born in Brighton,
England, in 1958. He studied at Eastbourne
College of Art and then worked in advertising for
15 years before becoming a full-time artist. He
has illustrated many children's nonfiction books.

Series Creator:
David Salariya was born in Dundee,
Scotland. He has illustrated a wide range of
books and has created and designed many new
series for publishers both in the UK and overseas.
In 1989, he established The Salariya Book
Company. He lives in Brighton with his wife,
illustrator Shirley Willis, and their son, Jonathan.

Editor:
Sophie Izod

Editorial Assistant:
Mark Williams

PAPER FROM
SUSTAINABLE
FORESTS

© The Salariya Book Company Ltd MMXVII
No part of this publication may be reproduced in whole or in
part, or stored in a retrieval system, or transmitted in any form or
by any means, electronic, mechanical, photocopying, recording,
or otherwise, without written permission of the publisher. For
information regarding permission, write to the copyright holder.

Published in Great Britain in 2017 by
The Salariya Book Company Ltd
25 Marlborough Place, Brighton BN1 1UB

ISBN-13: 978-0-531-23837-0 (lib. bdg.) 978-0-531-23159-3 (pbk.)

All rights reserved.
Published in 2017 in the United States
by Franklin Watts
An imprint of Scholastic Inc.

A CIP catalog record for this book is available
from the Library of Congress.

Printed and bound in China.
Printed on paper from sustainable sources.

1 2 3 4 5 6 7 8 9 10 R 26 25 24 23 22 21 20 19 18 17

SCHOLASTIC, FRANKLIN WATTS, and associated logos are
trademarks and/or registered trademarks of Scholastic Inc.

You Wouldn't Want to Be Tutankhamen!

Written by
David Stewart

Illustrated by
David Antram

Created and designed by
David Salariya

A Mummy Who Really Got Meddled With

Franklin Watts®
An Imprint of Scholastic Inc.

Contents

Introduction

It is around the mid-14th century BC and times are difficult in ancient Egypt. Your father, Pharaoh Akhenaten, has been ruling over Egypt for many years. For centuries society has barely changed, following the regular ebbing and flowing of the Nile. But recently, Akhenaten has introduced changes to Egyptian life and religion that are sending shockwaves throughout the civilization.

You are the royal prince, Tutankhaten, and one day you will be a pharaoh, too, but at the moment you are just a child. The discovery of your tomb more than 3,000 years later, in 1922, will make you the most famous pharaoh in the world.

Every summer, rain from the highlands of Ethiopia makes the River Nile swell up to flood its banks. The floodwater, full of rich, black silt, creates fertile strips of land on either side of the river where crops can grow.

Meet the Family

You live at a time in Egyptian history called "The New Kingdom." It was during this period that the Egyptian Empire was at its height of power and wealth. Enormous supplies of gold were being mined in the newly reconquered deserts to the east of the River Nile. Gold was described as being as "plentiful as dirt" in Egypt. Your family is rather complicated. Like all pharaohs of ancient Egypt, your father, king Akhenaten, has many wives. His great royal wife and queen is the beautiful Nefertiti. Your mother is believed to have been Kiya, one of his minor wives. Nefertiti and Akhenaten have six daughters, your half-sisters.

I was the first pharaoh to issue news bulletins.

Amenhotep III

Queen Nefertiti

The name Nefertiti means "my beautiful one has come." It is unlikely that Nefertiti is of royal blood. Her father is thought to be a high official called Ay who will one day rule as pharaoh after your death.

Grandparents

Queen Tiye

YOUR GRANDPARENTS are Amenhotep III and Queen Tiye. Amenhotep became king at around the age of 12 with his mother acting as regent. Tiye was the daughter of a military officer.

King Akhenaten

Queen Nefertiti

Sigh . . . a son and heir at last.

Handy Hint

A boy's prospects are better: at this time in Egypt pharaohs needed sons to rule after them. Your father had six daughters until your birth.

Smenkhkare?

Kiya

Tutankhaten

The Mysterious Smenkhkare

WHO WAS SMENKHKARE? Many Egyptologists think that Smenkhkare was your brother but others think that Nefertiti became known as Smenkhkare.

A New Religion

THE ANCIENT EGYPTIANS worship many gods, each protecting a different aspect of their lives. Some gods protect homes and cities. There are river gods, gods of wind and weather, sky gods, and a god to make the crops grow.

Your father thinks that the people are wrong to worship so many gods. He believes that there should be only one god—Aten (the sun disk), creator of everything. Akhenaten adopts this new religion and closes the temples where the old gods were worshipped. The ordinary people are dismayed and the powerful priests at the temples no longer have any work.

Horus

Thoth

Osiris

Isis

Ra

Hathor

Anubis

Akhetaten, the New City

NEW TEMPLES are built to Aten and a new capital city is established to replace Thebes (modern Luxor). It is called Akhetaten, which means "horizon of the sun." The site of the new capital is chosen because the cliffs nearby are shaped like the hieroglyphic word for "horizon," through which the sun god is "reborn" every morning.

The old gods will seek vengeance for this!

TWO TEMPLES are built in the heart of the new city. Like other Egyptian temples, they consist of a series of smaller courtyards leading to a shrine. In a traditional temple, this would lead to an enclosed shrine, but Aten's sun rays cannot be enclosed, so the courtyards are open. Offerings are made to the god and the courtyards are piled high with fruits, vegetables, birds, and other animals.

Childhood in the New City

The gold is like the rising sun.

You were born in the new city Akhetaten (now known as Amarna). Like other children from noble families, you are raised in the women's quarter of the palace. Education is highly valued and schools are part of the temple and government offices. Royal children have their own school within the palace. Boys start school at the age of five and the first thing they are taught to write is the *hieratic* script used for official documents. Older students learn to draw hieroglyphs that are used in religious texts.

Go for Gold!

THE WINDOW OF APPEARANCES. From this window the pharaoh showers his loyal subjects with gold as a symbol of the divine light of the sun. Your father also rewards his supporters with houses and even tombs for the nobility.

Well Fed

WHEN YOU were an infant, you had a nurse called Maia. She nursed you and treated you as her own child. You do not suffer from any of the common childhood illnesses.

Handy Hint

Practice and remember lots of different names. Pharaohs have names that describe the person as well as their role as ruler. For example, Rameses the Great.

Brushes

Hieroglyphs

Writing boxes

PRINCELY LEARNING. As you grow older, you are sent to a school especially for princes and sons of important nobles. The school is attached to one of the palaces. In the morning you concentrate on writing. In the afternoon you practice riding and shooting with a bow and arrow, skills important for warfare as well as hunting.

Your "Hometown"

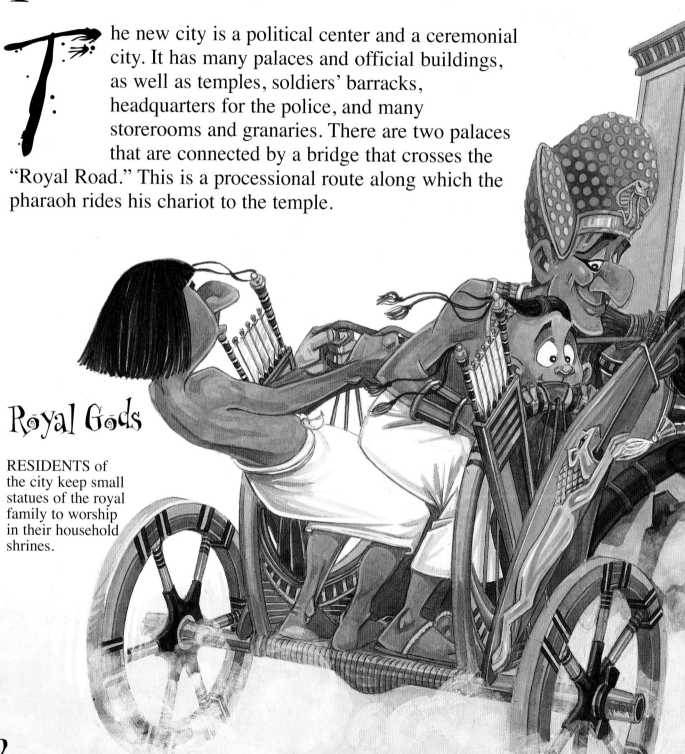

The new city is a political center and a ceremonial city. It has many palaces and official buildings, as well as temples, soldiers' barracks, headquarters for the police, and many storerooms and granaries. There are two palaces that are connected by a bridge that crosses the "Royal Road." This is a processional route along which the pharaoh rides his chariot to the temple.

Royal Gods

RESIDENTS of the city keep small statues of the royal family to worship in their household shrines.

Feasting

ORDINARY PEOPLE have simple diets consisting mainly of bread, vegetables, and beans. As a prince you enjoy meat, fish, cakes, beer, and wine—nothing but the best for you!

Palaces of Mud

The city is planned on a large scale. It encloses an area of 77 square miles and has a population estimated to be more than 20,000. Its palaces and houses are built of mud brick hardened in the sun. Only the temples are made from stone.

13

The Pharaoh Is Dead

Nefertiti–The Queen Who Became King!

Like other royalty, Queen Nefertiti has a confusing collection of royal titles and names. She is promoted over time from being a queen (chief wife to your father, Akhenaten), to a co-regent, so when Akhenaten dies, she becomes pharaoh.

n 1335 BC your father dies. Smenkhkare becomes pharaoh, but was Smenkhkare in charge? Ay, the grand vizier and Nefertiti's father, still holds his position of great power behind the throne. Over time, the traditional gods are reinstated. Gradually Akhenaten's name is removed from all monuments and the Aten temples are dismantled. The temple stones are re-used for other more traditional building projects.

Nefertiti becomes queen

She then becomes Neferneferuaten Nefertiti

Who later becomes co-regent Ankhkheprure

Then as co-regent she becomes ruler Pharaoh Ankhkheprure Smenkhkare

My name is Pentju, pharaoh's chief doctor.

Plague in Egypt?

A GREAT PLAGUE SWEEPS through Egypt at the time of Akhenaten's death and other members of your family also die around this time. The priests and followers of the old gods said that the plague was sent as a punishment because your father abandoned them. They use this as an excuse to go back to worshipping these gods after your father's death.

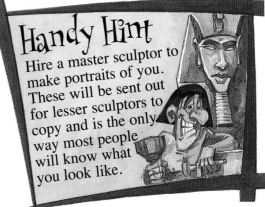

Handy Hint

Hire a master sculptor to make portraits of you. These will be sent out for lesser sculptors to copy and is the only way most people will know what you look like.

Looks like we're in for a queen as pharaoh!

DID CAPTURED PRISONERS bring the plague to Egypt?

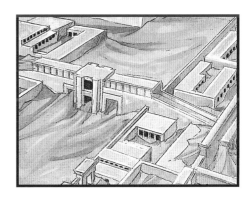

ABANDONED AND FORGOTTEN, sand gradually covers the once-magnificent city.

Long Live the Pharaoh!

In 1333 BC, at the age of nine, you become pharaoh. At your coronation, the priests set the crowns of Egypt on your head. At first you are too young to be a real ruler, so you are helped by plenty of advisors. Ay, Akhenaten's grand vizier; and Horemheb, the commander of the army, make decisions for you. Your father was preoccupied with religious reform and had neglected ruling his country, so many temples and cities have fallen into decay.

YOU HAVE TO BE trained to become a warrior leader. You will need to learn how to drive a chariot and to master other skills like archery and the use of weapons.

Tutankhaten, now Tutankhamen

Married

AS PHARAOH YOU MUST marry your older half-sister Ankhesenpaaten, whose name is changed to Ankhesenamen. Adopting these names signals the royal family's return to the old gods.

YOU CONTINUE THE work of restoring the old religion and rebuilding temples that Nefertiti had set in motion before Akhenaten's death. Anyone who dares to mention the Aten is punished. You change your name from Tutankhaten to Tutankhamen. This shows that you are now a faithful worshipper of Amen.

Not All Work

As pharaoh you are not just a mighty ruler, your people see you as a living god. This means that you have many religious duties to perform. You take part in religious ceremonies at the temples, say prayers, and make offerings to the gods so that past pharaohs will not be forgotten. The most important religious festival is the feast of Opet, which takes place once a year in Thebes when the Nile floods. Statues of the gods are taken by boat to the Temple of Luxor at Karnak. The procession has drummers, dancers, and acrobats. The gloomy festival of the god Osiris in the fourth month is when Egypt goes into mourning for the death of Osiris. After several days, priests announce that Osiris has risen from the dead and the festival becomes a celebration.

HUNTING IN THE DESERT is for the very wealthy. Your bow is inscribed with two hieroglyphs meaning you are the "possessor of a strong arm."

Your Favorite Game

SENET IS A BOARD GAME played on a rectangular board divided into squares. Casting-sticks are used to see who gets the highest score. You have four boards.

You have won the squares of "happiness" and "beauty."

18

Hunting in the Marshes

YOU ENJOY HUNTING in the marshes. Birds are trapped in nets or hunted using throw-sticks. Hunters sometimes use tame geese as a decoy, calling wild geese toward them. Specially trained dogs and cats are sometimes used to fetch the birds that have been hit with the throw-stick. Beware hunting hippos and crocodiles—they are very dangerous!

Handy Hint

Don't let the commander of the army become too powerful.

Not just the army, I'm in charge of trading missions and building works.

Got you!

Sudden Death

You die suddenly and unexpectedly in your late teens. The cause of your death is still unknown. Did you die from a blow to the head? Did Ay and Horemheb have anything to do with your death in their quest for power? Or was it simply an infection that set in after you broke your leg?

> Ah! Pharaoh at last!

Unfinished Paintings

> . . . but a funeral to arrange . . . quickly.

THE PAINTINGS in the tomb are unfinished. The artist recreates a scene of baboons that he has done in your unfinished official tomb.

THE LID of your sarcophagus cracks because the foot-shaped end of your outer coffin is too high. The lid is removed, the coffin leveled, the lid replaced, and the crack filled with plaster.

After your death, Ay becomes pharaoh and is in charge of the arrangements for your burial. The tomb chosen for you is very small and was probably built for someone else of much lower rank than you. Your sudden death at such a young age means that your official tomb remains unfinished.

Handy Hint

Your tomb needs to be well stocked with food for the well being of your "Ka."

I can have the tomb that was started for Tutankhamen.

Cracked Sarcophagus

Crack!

Beaten-up Shrine

No one's looking, give it a thump!

Whack!

THE PANELS for the shrine enclosing the coffins are banged into place roughly with mallets, damaging the decorated surfaces.

Dried and Wrapped

The preservation of an ancient Egyptian's body through mummification is essential for a happy afterlife. The *ka,* or life-force of the deceased, is believed to remain in the tomb and receives offerings of food and drink. The *ba,* which represents the deceased personality, can leave the tomb to maintain contact between the worlds of the living and the dead. It is vital that your body does not decay if your ba and ka are to flourish, so the embalmers do everything to ensure that your body is perfectly preserved for the afterlife.

THE BOOK OF THE DEAD is a guidebook to help you through any problems in the underworld.

Ka

Ba

ANUBIS is often identified by the word "sab" which means "jackal." This is possibly because Egyptians would have noticed jackals around areas where burials took place.

It takes 515 feet of linen strips to wrap a body.

THE JACKAL MASK is worn by a priest or an embalmer playing the role of Anubis.

Handy Hint
Watch out, Tutankhamen! Embalmers are around!

Your sternum and much of your rib cage are removed and your chest is stuffed with bundles of cloth.

399 pounds of natron are used to dry a body out.

What Is a Mummy?

A MUMMY is the result of a long process. The body is washed first and then the brain (which is thought to be of little importance) is pulled out through the nose and thrown away. Next the liver, lungs, stomach, and intestines are removed. Special jars are used to store these organs, which are embalmed separately. The heart is kept with the body because it is believed that the dead person would need it to be judged in the afterlife. The body is then cleaned out and covered with natron, a type of powdery salt that dries it out. After 35 to 40 days, the body is dried out and ready to be wrapped in about twenty layers of bandages. The complete process takes 70 days.

The Valley of the Kings

n early March 1323 BC, your funeral takes place in The Valley of the Kings, on the west bank of the River Nile, the land of the dead. Like all wealthy Egyptians, you will take with you everything you need for a happy afterlife. Your sudden death has caused your burial to be a rushed and haphazard affair using old funeral equipment. Ay takes your widow as his wife to secure his claim to the throne.

THE VALLEY OF THE KINGS contains many tombs of pharaohs from the New Kingdom. Tombs cut into the solid rock were favored after the repeated lootings of the pyramids.

No Weighing of the Heart for You!

IN DEATH, pharaohs are believed to join the sun god traveling across the sky in a ship. But non-royals are judged before Osiris and their hearts are weighed against the Feather of Truth. If found free from sin, the deceased is admitted to the realms of the dead. The monster Ammut (a combination of a crocodile, lion, and hippo) waits in the judgment hall to eat the heart of those who fail the test.

AY PERFORMS The Opening of the Mouth ceremony. Egyptians believe that this returns the five senses to the mummy. With its senses restored, the deceased could enjoy the food offerings left in the tomb.

Handy Hint
Watch out, Tutankhamen! Embalmers are around!

Yours is the only royal mummy to have been hung upside down during the mummification process.

PRIESTS, courtiers, and servants follow your coffin.

I heard he was murdered . . .

I heard it was just an infection in his leg . . .

YOUR BODY LIES within its three coffins and is dragged on a sledge toward your tomb.

Tomb Raiders

Your tomb is sealed and you're left to enjoy eternity in peace . . . but not for long because robbers break into your tomb twice. Ay tries to remove all evidence of your father's and your reigns. He replaces your names with his own on many of the monuments you had built. When Ay dies four years after you, Horemheb succeeds him as pharaoh. Sand slowly covers the entrance to your tomb, and over time, your reign is forgotten along with your father's.

THE ENTRANCE to your tomb is plastered over, and seals marked with prayers for protection from the gods are stamped into the wet plaster.

You've been going in there again and again — too much is missing.

THE FATE OF captured robbers was gruesome: they were first beaten on the soles of their feet with a stick before being impaled slowly on a sharpened stake.

Lost and Found

Your tomb lies undisturbed for 3,200 years. Then in 1922, English archaeologist Howard Carter makes the most famous archaeological discovery in the world: your tomb. Carter was employed by English aristocrat Lord Carnarvon. His discovery makes you the most famous pharaoh of all. Your reign was too short to make much of an impression, but the treasures from your tomb amaze and inspire the world. You have achieved immortality despite Ay's attempts to erase you.

Cursed?

THE DEATH OF Lord Carnarvon four months after the opening of the tomb gave rise to the idea of the curse of the pharaohs. At the time of his death, all the lights in Cairo blacked out, and at the same time in England, Carnarvon's three-legged dog Suzy howled and dropped dead. The death of anyone remotely connected with your tomb was then linked to the curse. However, Howard Carter survived for another seventeen years, completing his task of clearing your tomb and dying in 1939. He died of natural causes.

You Wouldn't Want to Be Tutankhamen – Not Only Mummified . . . Carbonized Too!

CARTER BLAMES the bad state your mummy is in on the embalmers. He says that the use of too much embalming oil may have caused your mummy to start carbonizing, or turning into charcoal. Hot knives are used to melt the resin that holds your mummy in its coffin. Then you are left out in the hot desert sun. The damage done to your body is disguised when it is laid on a tray of sand to be photographed with enough sand not only to support your remains, but to hide the fact that you had been taken apart.

PEOPLE from all over the world visit your tomb.

Handy Hint For a Peaceful Eternity

Avoid being found if you want eternal peace. Immortality means that your tomb has been invaded, your belongings taken along with your dignity when you're unwrapped and x-rayed.

I don't believe it – this coffin is solid gold and it's inlaid with gemstones.

Glossary

Ammut A demon of the underworld who attended the "weighing of the heart" test and ate the heart of anybody who failed it.

Akhenaten The father of Tutankhamen.

Akhetaten The capital city built by Akhenaten and later abandoned after his death.

Ankhesenamen Daughter of Nefertiti and Akhenaten and wife to Tutankhamen.

Anubis The jackal-headed god of embalming.

Ba One of the three spirits released when someone died. It represented the person's character or personality.

Bitumen A tar-like substance used in the mummification process.

Book of the Dead A collection of spells and prayers left in tombs to help the dead in the underworld.

Canopic jars The set of four jars in which the embalmed lungs, stomach, liver, and intestines were stored.

Embalming The practice of preserving dead bodies.

Hieroglyphs The ancient Egyptian writing system that consists of pictures representing sounds. They were written both horizontally and vertically.

Howard Carter English archaeologist who discovered Tutankhamen's tomb in 1922.

Grand vizier A high-ranking official in the Egyptian court.

Ka The ka was a person's life force. When the person died, their ka lived on in their mummy.

Mummy An embalmed body wrapped in linen bandages. The word "mummy" comes from the Persian word *mummiya*, meaning pitch or bitumen. Some Egyptian mummies blackened over time and gave rise to the incorrect belief that bitumen was the embalming agent used.

Natron A form of natural salt used to dry out the body during the mummification process.

New Kingdom The period from 1550 to 1070 BC during which Egypt was ruled by pharaohs.

Regent Someone who rules either with or instead of the true ruler. This is normally because the ruler is too young to rule alone.

Sarcophagus A large outer coffin, usually made of stone.

Senet An ancient Egyptian board game popular at the time of Tutankhamen.

Sledge A strong, heavy sled.

Throw-stick A type of boomerang used for hunting.

Tutankhaten The birth name of Tutankhamen—it means "beloved of Aten." He changed his name to Tutankhamen ("beloved of Amen") when he adopted the old gods' religion again.

Index